THE MOON & HER SUNFLOWERS

A COLLECTION OF MUSINGS

Victoria Jade Moss

BookLeaf Publishing

India | USA | UK

Presentation by *BookLeaf Publishing*
Web: www.bookleafpub.com
E-mail: info@bookleafpub.com
ISBN: 9789358361476

First edition 2021

This book is dedicated to all those who read

a poem and go "...huh, I don't get it."

CONTENTS

PREFACE

*Thirty-one poems in thirty-one
days. A challenge it did indeed
prove to be.
As I discovered, writing furiously and in
disarray, words much like feelings are not
always so simple to convey
and creativity, much like love, cannot be
forced.
An effort should be made all the same,
otherwise having passion would be for
nought.*

I.

My soul is a star
my light will one day fade.
Destined I'll succumb to a blackhole,
a mysterious void in a universe
in which I never quite found my place.

Oblivion, it seems, is man's greatest fear
to never be enough,
or remembered,
or know where they will go from here

I, for one, find comfort in what cannot be proven
for then no one can say I won't one day
fly in the wake of a shooting star,
dance along the Milky Way
or count the craters while skipping on the moon.

To exist in the darkness
that has never scared me
but has offered
a home,
 a sanctuary

Oblivion is nothing to fear, you see?
It is whatever you dream to be peace
It is wherever you believe *your place* to be

- ***Oblivion***

II.

Petals of sunshine,
texture like silk
Centre of chocolate seeds
so decadent,
the sight so sweet

A gift of summer
drawn to the sun itself
They grow and grow and grow
as if trying to return home
The leaves green like grass in spring
such joy they do bring

How well they weather
the absence of rain
only needing light to sustain
Gathered in fields
together they bloom
Their presence so beautiful
a long-lived love of mine, it's true

Every time I look upon a sunflower
I'm reminded of you
- Sunflowers

III.

The children at school were cruel
the girl didn't understand why
She was always nice, always kind
Although at times a little shy.

The parents often yelled
no matter how hard she tried.
Her room was kept clean,
her chores attended to
and was *always* ready on time.
But still the parents raged
never pleased with the effort she made

The girl never let the bullies,
or her parents get her down
for she had what no one else did,
an invisible pixie that followed her around.
It would perch on her shoulder
sometimes hide in her pocket,
leave her pixie dust on whatever
her tiny hands touched.

The pixie was the girl's greatest friend
She would sit with her at recess and at the dinner
table where the parents would yell again
The pixie would comfort the girl,
let her know she would be okay
and was the only one to give her praise.

She would tell her fairy-tales
the ones always believed a farce.
Every story was charming and
would often make the girl laugh.

The pixie offered the greatest advice,
said the kind things others never did.
'To this world you are a gift.
You are strong, and you are resilient.
You don't need mine; you are your own magic.'

The girl would one day reach the age
where she would no longer need her invisible friend.
But for now, come each bedtime
the pixie was always there.
Would whisper that she was loved
and to *'sleep tight'*
and then she would stay with the girl
all through the night.

- Resilience

IV.

Hell is not a fiery realm where the devil tortures
wicked souls
It is a threat to those who seek to harm others
A comfort to those who have already been harmed
A promise that peace is a gift their monsters will
never know

Hell is the construct of one's mind.
For what is worse than spending eternity with
nowhere to hide from the worst parts of
yourself?
The parts that are
contempt,
jealousy,
greed
being haunted by your darkest
thoughts, and most painful memories.

Hell is born of hate.
Resentment and grudges, the Masters of the Gate.
Hate is poison, it mars the soul
It eats away at those quick to despise,
a wasteland where the embittered reside

Until the anger you feel has been lifted
Hell is what you'll continue to go through
For the torture, you see, is self-inflicted because
the *devil* you dance with, is *you.*

- Devil

V.

Such a beautiful thing
to glimpse the wild horses.
Through the fields they race the wind,
drink the trickling water of the springs

Graze beneath a golden sky,
gallop and frolic to their own delight,
rearing and bucking in reckless abandon.
No soul would dare attempt to tame them

With no restrictions and no reins
in wide open spaces
on the grassy plains
where the wildflowers grow,
where freedom is home
That is where the wild horses roam
- *Wild*

"Sunshine's Paddock" - Thelma Lesslie

VI.

A small act of kindness to a stranger,
a slight smile when you pass one by,
can lift another's spirits
when they are finding it hard not to cry.
A brief moment of friendly exchange
may be enough to help someone feel less estranged.
Ease one's doubt in the goodness of mankind
where compassion too often falls to the
wayside of pride.
Ego is not worth the price of
hurting a heart already in strife.
Living with empathy and humanity costs nothing
when half of man's problems can be solved just
through loving
- Compassion

VII.

I have tolerated the treachery of trust misgiven
and weathered feelings misplaced.
I have outlasted the night
and beat the sun to the east.

I have kept to the shoreline,
respected the ocean and its boundaries.
I have bloomed where others withered,
dug my roots in deep while they fled

I have worshipped midnight
like most do a sun-bathed day.
She gives me silence
because words do not belong.
Words they too often lie
and its words that have always led me wrong
- ***Words***

VIII.

Precious baby boy
Mummy and Daddy's little man
wrapped in blue swaddle,
a matching bottle in hand.

His nursery a theme of construction trucks,
hammers, and nails.
All toys in greens, blues, browns, and yellows.

Over the years there were racing cars,
spaceships and rockets.
Pirates, zombies, toy guns, cops, and robbers
They quickly became all the things he hates.

So, each Christmas or birthday he faked excitement
by putting on a happy face.
An entire childhood of presents gone to waste

All because the boy liked to sing and dance around,
spend time in the garden
where no one could see him wear his toy crown.

Instead, he got army figurines
and superhero clothes.
A baseball glove,
a cricket bat,
a football to throw.
Even as he grew older,
he preferred to stay and read inside.

He didn't like the roughhousing or
how it sometimes made him cry.
The others would just say *'man up'*
and *'it's all part of being a guy'.*

Because boys don't get to have pretty little things,
to play dress up and have tea parties,
chase fairies or wear butterfly wings.

His entire life he felt left out;
always out of place.
But now he knows it's good to be different
and that he never has to fake.
To himself, he will forever be true,
even when they say that
'boys will be boys'

Well, this *boy* is sick of *blue*.
- Blue

IX.

It is said it will come for us all
it will sink its claws in deep
to steal breath and heartbeats
stake a claim and scatter souls like morning mist

It is said the pain is ephemeral
It will ebb, increase then fade
At the end both light and darkness will fill its void;
fill *our lungs,*
our hollow chests,
our veins.

It is said to be fleeting, or to last an eternity
It is quick or bides its time.
A road too travelled and a path not yet explored.

Is it love?
Or is it death?
Both will come
to curse or to gift.

-Eternity

X.

On transparent wings
they take flight at twilight
A woodland gift of spring
A teensy shimmering life

Flash, flash, flash

Wicked femme fatale
hypnotic signals
and poised to attack
The males all fall under her spell

Little buzzing lanterns
Bioluminescent tiny wonders
Dazzling all bystanders,
Aglow in their caverns

Pretty little lightning bug
How grand to shine so bright?
How can one be glum
with such an oddity in sight?

Not a mere beetle
but a beacon in the night

Follow a firefly
And let it give you *light*
-Glow

XI.

My heart is poison
I warned you not to taste.
Trying to claim it is a dangerous feat
and will prove to be your greatest mistake
Like those before you, you're blinded by my red
flags; the ones that draw you near.
Their colour pretty as roses
but words sharp as barbed thorns
all the ones you pretend not to hear.

I have built my walls for a reason
neither I nor them will fall
You'll soon enough realise
the words I spoke were true
and you'll wish to have never met me at all.

So, despite what you believe you can conquer
and the parts of me you think you can change
I shall warn you once again
this heart of mine is poison
One prick of its thorns and yours will be too

You are no exception to the pain that I inflict.
You'll break just like the others
because, to me, love is a sin I'll never commit

-Poison

XII.

The girl and the moon had an understanding. The moon would not question why the girl stayed awake while the rest of her world slumbered. And the girl would not question why some nights the moon struggled to share its light at all.

- Understanding

XIII.

When *it* becomes too much
and the voices grow loud
Ground yourself

Find that place,
that scent,
that sound

When your dreams turn dark,
the memories overwhelm
Calm yourself.
 Imagine that happy place,
that comforting scent,
that peaceful sound.

The ones that settle the churning thoughts,
 your racing pulse
and fills your aching chest with warmth
Close your eyes.
Conjure it in your mind.
Feel its serenity, its peace, take a moment to
realign.

When you need a lifeline
a place where you can hide
be safe in your special space
where no enemy can breach, no worry can reach

It's here where you will heal

from the old wounds you still feel
when you imagine

that place,
that scent,
that sound

Where all that was loved and lost can still be found

-Trauma

XIV.

There once were sunflowers that bloomed along a
chain linked fence.
They ran beside the gravel road to the property's
entrance—the children's favourite place
where possibilities were endless.

The property was immense so
many places to hide.
With sheds and wheat bins full of grain
the rusty steel insides made the perfect slide.
There were great big tractors and forklifts,
a quaint little house nestled amongst
the towering gum trees
where the kookaburras would come to feed.

To the children the best thing of all
were the stacks of wooden planks,
wide as they were tall.
Splintered and unstable
a pile of rotted timber left to decay
but to the children it was a castle,
their favourite place to play.

Till dark they would climb,
explore and create grand games, daring quests
Imagining worlds only they could see.
They would run through rogue wheat stems,
jump over old machinery,
dance among the draping branches
of the weeping willow trees.

Before too long the seasons passed, as did the years.
There became less games to play
and quests to take.
The pencil marks on the doorframe —
the ones that measured their height —
like the carpet in the quaint little house,
were no longer quite as bright.
The time had come to say goodbye
to the small town and Country Life.

Behind closed eyes or in the back of her mind
the girl still remembers
dirt lanes,
tall stems with yellow petals
cartwheels,
swing sets,
and an imagination that would never settle.

So, although the children have grown,
their castle has long since perished
with no more willows to hide in or grain to sift,
the memories remain to be forever cherished

The ones of splinters in fingers
and sunflowers on a chain linked fence
It was the age of innocence
-Innocence

XV.

The drawings on her skin tell
a story

Each line a time there was a
win but no glory

A battle where she conquered a demon
which has consumed too many others whole

She is not weak or
seeking attention
She is a *survivor*
She is a *warrior*

Worthy of love and affection
- Worthy

XVI.

I hate the morning sun,
it never seems to transition quite right.
The timing and intensity are always wrong.

I hate the birds that interrupt the dawn,
heralding the awkward sunrise.
Perhaps what I hate is that, come morning,
I am alone.

The companionship of the moon has left me
taking with it my dreams.
It is my greatest love
for we share a truth:
we both come alive in darkness.
There is a peace.
A stillness.
A realm of inspiration and beauty.

In the night, I can trust
because days can be both bright and gloomy,
but the night is always dark.
- Trust

XVII.

Weathered skin kissed by the sun.
Hands a little shaky and less sure than before.
Through the years she never imagined
the happiness she would find kneeling in a garden.

Tired joints creak like the door of the back porch
but still, she works elbow deep in dirt every day.
Not just a plot of loam but a memoir of sorts,
a journal penned in the garden's bed

The flowers she plants extensions of herself
for every *seed* she sows is a thought once gleaned.
Each *iris* planted is a memory from days long gone.
Every *poppy*, someone lost and cherished.
The *roses*, unrequited loves.
The *lilies*, her children now grown,
lilacs, a tribute to her youth

The cobbled path through the backyard
a generation of milestones.
Dedicated bees, dreams recognised and pursued.

Butterflies, a hope once lost then born anew.

The life story of the old lady written in the reverently
tended soil
one just as *beautiful*
and *rich*
and *full*
as her garden in bloom.

- Bloom

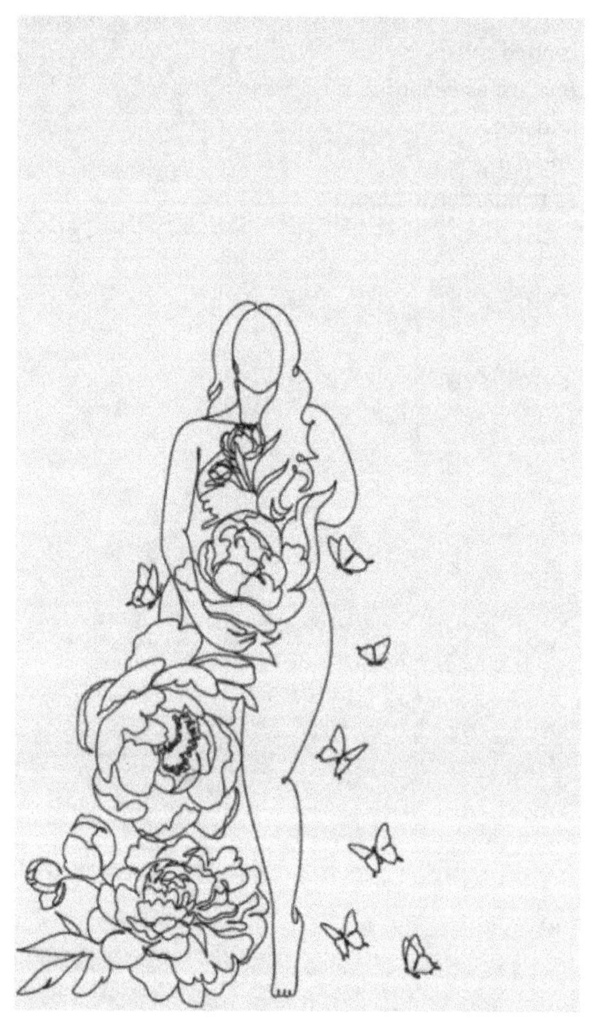

XVIII.

It is pink and red with specks of black.
It tastes sweet then sour,
till it turns to ash.
It all happens so fast and in slow motion.
A car-crash.
A roller coaster.
So much emotion.

'We should take a breather,' you say 'Get some air'
'Break up,' I suggest
'I never loved you anyway,' you declare.
Shouting follows,
tears are shed
then, 'Let me show how much I care'
'Forgive me,' we both plea.
A toxic cycle
A fight we are only doomed to repeat.

It's subtle,
a statement,
a grand affair.
Burns bright and fizzles
fast.
Over years,
soon becomes a burden to bear.

I wish the hurt would go away
'Please don't leave,' you beg,
'please tell me you'll stay.'

Then a solution!
A vow!
It will keep us happy for now.
On bended knee,
comes a 'Marry me,'
'I do' you say
'Till death,' we swear.
Smiles and laughter
until months after
'No wait! Don't go, things will get better.'
But it will never change
despite the rings we wear.

Dinner left uneaten,
calls gone unanswered,
texts left on read,
an empty side of the bed.

At first, it's one night,
'Don't wait up,' you tell me,
'I'm out with the guys,'
Less time together, more spent apart.
And then excuses begin to start

'They need me to work again,' you explain,
'Over the weekend as well'.
'But you're never home,' I complain
'You don't understand,' you yell, 'My boss is giving
me hell.'

'Is there someone else?' I fret
'Don't think that,' you say,
'you have no reason to doubt.'

Picture perfect.
A fairy-tale.
A couple for others to envy.
Two people so deeply in love
but like the house they once shared,
their hearts are now empty.

Two different lives lived, one
kept secret.
It's true what they say,
'The first cut is the deepest.'
The pinks and reds of love
can no longer be seen
like our marriage
they were only *temporary*

Along with this poem and its staggered flow
some people, together, just don't go.
- Separation

XIX.

I love her endlessly
she, who has been a companion
throughout the years.
A comfort,
a silent surety.

I owe her my words,
my stories
and madness

She is my greatest muse

She is night eternal

and I am ephemeral.

- *Ephemeral*

XX.

In the morning, we wake
to an ivory blanket of snowflakes
the hands of winter take hold,
embracing us in it's cold.

At times a blinding tempest
but in it, I find a stillness.
The world, it falls away
when home on a snow day.

The fire, it roars filling the room with its warmth
but I remain still, content in the serenity
the snowstorm brings.

The flakes, although in a flurry,
I am in no hurry.
So, I stay snuggled by the window
finding beauty and a stillness in the snow.

- Stillness

XXI.

Still, I'm trying to navigate
the dark side of my heart
It's nothing more than a frozen tundra
one I long to break through
hoping it will be the day I find my way back;
to once again feel the sun upon my face
and no longer the shadow of you in my past,
shrouding me in all I fought to escape
- *Shadow*

XXII.

Seated on a wooden bench
woollen scarf and gloves.
Autumn kissed branches
swaying above.
Watch a leaf as it falls
adrift on its journey
dropping from trees so tall
without a worry.

Vacation — fun it may be —
is well and truly gone.
Autumn, now the season of reality
Summer is no more.
Coffee in hand,
time to leave the park
return to the desk and paperwork,
hopefully make it home before dark.

- Reality

XXIII.

Time is the true bearer of responsibility
It will forge mountains and fortify forests.
With absence, it can make the heart grow fonder
and heal one heavy with hurt

Time lowers and raises the sun,
it will hang the moon and dot the sky with stars.
It ages
wine,
cheese,
 pages of a book.

Time fills eyes with wisdom, wariness, and prejudice.
It will border them with deep lines and thinning skin.
It must bring maturity, knowledge, and logic to all
those who endure it.

Time has a price and is priceless
for all that time grants us it is both
coveted and taken for granted.
A blessing and a cruel joke,
both a prisoner and a prosecutor.

Time will blossom but too it will wilt,
Just as we are born and just as we die.
Time is the master of life.

       - Time

XXIV.

You hardly ever say '*I love you*'
Instead, you say, 'Have fun, be safe.
Drive carefully tonight, it's pouring rain.
Be sure to take a coat, you don't want to get sick
again'

You tell me, 'Don't forget to take your vitamins,
I know they always help,'
Or ask 'Have you eaten today? You look a little pale.
Are you feeling okay?'

You notice when feeling I'm down and do
what you can to make it better.
You tell me, 'Why don't you get some sun;
fresh air will do you good.
Make the best of this nice weather.'

Each night you say, 'Sweet dreams and sleep tight'
Every morning you greet me with 'hello'

You hardly ever say, '*I love you*'
Sometimes those three words
are not enough on their own.
To prove to someone how much you care a
declaration is not always needed
when you can show your love just by being there
- Declaration

XXV.

You cannot ignore how the sea does roar
when pulled in opposing directions
drowning with afflictions.
Conflicting rips demand she obey
unfeeling to the parts of her that are torn away.
The waves rage, screaming of her pain.

But on we watch and listen in vain
unable to help while she wars with herself
The darkness of the depths overwhelm
Such turmoil beneath the surface
Her wildness still not enough to deter us

The sea is not so different from you and me
All filled with uncertainty that pulls us underneath
such *suffering*,
such *strength*
 such a *magnificent sight;*
seeing her in all her might

Like the ocean we must try to tame our waves
and hold out for those calmer days

-Tame

XXVI.

Regret can be a bitter pill to swallow,
to suffer the consequences
of decisions now wished undone
Forgiveness is often slow to follow

So unfair it is that those with empathy
must endure such trials
over a simple lapse of judgment
good intentions gone awry

So unjust that the villains are the ones
free from the burden of guilt
never having to taste the bitterness of conscience or
to live in a cage regret has built.

- Cage

XXVII.

A broken heart is still a heart
even if pieces are missing
Use whatever you can to mend it,
no matter how unsightly

Bind the debris with staples,
string, coloured tape,
daisy chains and odd ribbons
Stuff the gaps with old newspaper scraps and
fill the cracks with glittered glue

Soon, others will see how your once broken heart
is now a work of art
and the beauty you created from rubble will
forever be *a piece of you*
- *Art*

XXVIII.

The sun has betrayed me
has shone its light
where none had the right to be

the world had not known of my misery
the night had kept it safe in the dark
where only She could see

Come day, it's all too clear
the tears that always stain
I tried to hide it,
guard what was only mine,
to tuck away the pain

I must ask the sun to show me kindness
and return me to the night

She will wrap me in her darkness
cradle me while I weep,
glitter stardust on my grief-streaked cheeks

The moon shall sing me a lullaby
and watch over me while I sleep

- Kindness

XXIX.

It's the little — seemingly insignificant — moments
that, over time, help soothe a soul long since in pain.

The unbridled laugh of a child which breaks through
the fog of your mind
The smell before the rain that eases
the ache in your bones
An elderly couple on a bench, proof of a lifelong love
A butterfly fluttering nearby catching your attention;
a sign of beauty in existence

All that is hurtful in the world falls away
leaving the peace and comfort of a moment
that filled your heart with something other than pain
—a promise that your soul
will one day be whole again.
- Insignificant

XXX.

Despite the sun shining more brightly, the moon never let that discourage her from changing tides and lighting pathways for hapless souls hiding in the night.

- Hiding

XXXI.

Who is she?
Who holds so many hearts and captivates great
minds?

She who has been the muse for such genius through
the centuries and shall do through all of time

She whose elegance artists try to capture with
strokes of a brush
Whom musicians serenade
 like one would a lover's touch

Poets write of her *beauty,*
her *sin,*
her *might.*

She who scientists study
and dedicate their lives.

Who is she?
The one who holds the sky, dictates time and date

She is *fire,*
rain,
a hurricane,
She is a *tidal wave.*

She whose tears cause monsoons,
and floods the land
Whose anger splits the earth,
buildings crumbling on demand
She whose screams with the force of a wind
man cannot withstand

She is life in its truest form

Death incarnate

She is the moon

The Mother of Nature

The greatest muse of man

She is *woman.*

-Empower

ACKNOWLEDGEMENT

Thank you to my parents, Vickie and John who suffered through some atrocious attempts at poetry while I fought through bouts of writer's block during this challenge. May you never have to hear another poem about the moon again.

Thanks to my Nanna, Shirley- any writing talent I have I got it from you.

Finally, to Alvira Publishing, BookLeaf Publishing and their teams for this opportunity.
(Side note: to a 'certain someone', no, that poem is not about you!)